ANIMAL SUPERPOWERS

AMAZING ANIMAL COMMUNICATORS

John Townsend

Raintree

Chicago, Illinois

D1314687

www.capstonepub.com
Visit our website to find out more information about Heinemann-Raintree books.

To order:

☎ Phone 800-747-4992

💻 Visit www.capstonepub.com to browse our catalog and order online.

© 2013 Raintree
an imprint of Capstone Global Library, LLC
Chicago, Illinois

All rights reserved. No part of this publication may be reproduced or transmitted in any form or by any means, electronic or mechanical, including photocopying, recording, taping, or any information storage and retrieval system, without permission in writing from the publisher.

Edited by Rebecca Rissman, Dan Nunn, and Catherine Veitch
Designed by Joanna Hinton-Malivoire
Picture research by Mica Brancic
Production by Victoria Fitzgerald

Originated by Capstone Global Library

Library of Congress Cataloging-in-Publication Data
Townsend, John
Amazing animal communicators / John Townsend.
—1st ed.
p. cm.—(Animal superpowers)
Includes bibliographical references and index.
ISBN 978-1-4109-4744-4 (hb)
ISBN 978-1-4109-4751-2 (pb) 1. Animal communication—Juvenile literature. 2. Animal communicators—Juvenile literature. I. Title.
 QL776.T69 2013
 591.59—dc23   2011041353

Printed and bound in the USA.
001559

Acknowledgments
We would like to thank the following for permission to reproduce photographs: Alamy: Arco Images GmbH, 26; Avalon Photos: Photoshot/JTB, 11, Photoshot/NHPA/ Gerry Cambridge, 25; Getty Images: Paul Nicklen, 18, 19; Nature Picture Library: TOM WALMSLEY, 21; Science Source: Christopher Swann, 23, Lena Untidt, 9, Steve Percival, 10; Shutterstock: Andrew Sutton, 22, Anke van Wyk, 15, bond girl, 5, Christopher Tan Teck Hean, 12, Danomyte, 29, David Grigg, 4, Fotochip, 8, Krzysztof Odziomek, 20, kyslynskahal, Cover, Michal Durinik, 7, noolwlee, 13, Steven R Smith, 24, Theodore Mattas, 14, worldswildlifewonders, 6, xlt974, 17, Zadiraka Evgenii, 16; SuperStock: Mint Images, 27

Every effort has been made to contact copyright holders of material reproduced in this book. Any omissions will be rectified in subsequent printings if notice is given to the publisher.

We would like to thank Michael Bright for his invaluable help in the preparation of this book.

Disclaimer
All the Internet addresses (URLs) given in this book were valid at the time of going to press. However, due to the dynamic nature of the Internet, some addresses may have changed, or sites may have changed or ceased to exist since publication. While the author and publisher regret any inconvenience this may cause readers, no responsibility for any such changes can be accepted by either the author or the publisher.

Some words are shown in bold, **like this**. You can find out what they mean by looking in the glossary.

Contents

Animals Can Be Superheroes!

Superheroes in stories communicate in special or secret ways. Many animals also use amazing tricks to communicate with each other. Read this book to find out which animals send and receive messages in super-amazing ways.

Super Warning

How can a small animal say, "Don't eat me"—without talking? Easy! It has bright colors, which make it look scary. Many animals give clear messages just by the way they look. Poison arrow frogs have bright colors that say, "Keep away— I'm deadly."

Did You Know?
Just one of these tiny South American frogs has enough **poison** to kill 10 people.

Super Dance

The way you move can say a lot about you. It is called body language. When a bee finds food, it uses body language to tell other bees. By doing a special dance, it shows them where to get **nectar** to make honey.

A bee's "waggle dance" is in a figure eight. The dance points other bees toward where there is food.

Super Light

Telling your friends where you are in the dark is easy if you can shine bright signals. Some insects do this with their flashing bodies. Glowworms are a type of beetle. Female glowworms light up to attract males and to warn **predators** to stay away.

Fireflies communicate at night by lighting up.

Super Messages

Ants living in large groups often have to get messages around their colony (home) in a hurry. They need to warn others of danger and tell them about food. Ants tap or feel each other with their **antennae** to pass on information.

Did You Know?

Ants' messages are often sent as smells and chemicals.

Super Signals

Elephants can keep in touch with other elephants from a few miles away by making a long-distance call! The elephants make very deep, low rumbles that other elephants can pick up with their huge ears, heads, and even trunks.

Did You Know?
Elephants feel **vibrations** from other elephants through the ground with their feet and the tips of their trunks.

Super Color

Some superheroes change color. Some animals can, too. Chameleons can change their skin color very quickly. When they blend in with their surroundings, their **camouflage** makes them almost **invisible** to **predators**.

Did You Know?
Bright colors say, "Let's fight," and pale colors say, "You win."

Super Display

Sailfish are super-fast fish. They also have other superpowers. When they go hunting together, their bodies become an amazing display of colors and patterns. This is how they communicate and avoid stabbing each other with their long spikes.

Did You Know?
A hunting sailfish raises its large **fin** like a sail. It can change color and flash.

fin

19

Super Talk

Dolphins are super-smart sea **mammals**. Dolphins use their own language to keep in touch underwater. Their "talk" uses patterns of squawks, whistles, clicks, and squeaks. They can pick up these signals over long distances with their super hearing.

Dolphins can quickly learn human commands and hand signals.

Super-Loud Talk

Whales "sing" their messages to each other across many miles of sea. This way of communicating helps them keep in touch with other whales when **migrating** across the ocean.

blue whale

The blue whale is the biggest whale, and its voice is the loudest—even louder than a jet engine!

Super Attraction

How can a female luna moth attract a partner? She sends her message with perfume. Through her smell signals, she attracts male moths from far away, even across a field of flowers.

luna moth

Super Show-Off

How can a male bird in a forest find a female partner? He has to put on a stunning show. Male lyrebirds are the superstars of the Australian forest. They copy other birdsong or sounds, including chainsaws and car alarms! If a female likes it, she comes running.

Male lyrebirds put on a dance show with their tail feathers to say, "Am I attractive enough?"

Quiz: Spot the Superhero!

Test your powers of observation and see if you can spot the superhero. You can find the answers on page 32, if you are really stuck!

1. Which of these animals can speak through dance?
a) a bee
b) a frog
c) an elephant

2. Which of these animals can flash light signals?
a) a moth
b) a dolphin
c) a firefly

3. Which of these animals can change color to give signals?

a) an ant

b) a chameleon

c) an elephant

4. Which of these animals can signal over a long distance?

a) a frog

b) a whale

c) an ant

5. Which of these animals can show off with song and dance?

a) a lyrebird

b) a dolphin

c) a moth

Glossary

antennae pair of movable sense organs on the head of an insect

camouflage hiding something by covering it up or changing the way it looks

fin thin, wing-like body part that a fish uses to help guide its movements

invisible unable to be seen

mammal warm-blooded animal that makes milk for its young

migrating moving from one region to another for feeding or breeding

nectar sweet liquid in flowers that is used by bees for making honey

poison substance that can cause death or harm

predator animal that hunts other animals

vibration trembling movement

Find Out More

Books

Arlon, Penelope. *DK First Animal Encyclopedia.*
New York: Dorling Kindersley, 2004.

Gilpin, Daniel. *Record-Breaking Animals* (Record
Breakers). New York: PowerKids, 2012.

Johnson, Jinny. *Amazing Animals* (Explorers).
New York: Kingfisher, 2012.

Websites

**kids.nationalgeographic.com/kids/stories/
animalsnature/dolphin-language**
Find out about the secret language of dolphins.

**www.sandiegozoo.org/animalbytes/
t-chameleon.html**
This Website has lots of information about
chameleons, including how and why they
change color.

Index

Answers: 1.a, 2.c, 3.b, 4.b, 5.a.